The Lord's Prayer

Jack Hayford

Our Father in Heaven
Hallowed be Your name
Your kingdom come
Your will be done
On earth as it is in heaven
Give us this day our daily bread
And forgive us our debts
As we forgive our debtors
And do not lead us into temptation
But deliver us from the evil one
For yours is the kingdom and the
Power and the glory forever. Amen

Matthew 6:9-13   NKJV

Personal Study Guide

Contents

Introduction

Welcome! You are about to embark on an exciting and spiritually rewarding journey. To help you maximize the lessons presented in this video, we've outlined some simple suggestions we hope will be helpful ...

1. Take personal notes. Your notes will help remind you of key points long after your viewing of the video.
2. Study all scripture references. Write down all scripture references and then study those scriptures in your personal time.
3. Ask questions: After viewing the video, ask questions on any parts of the video still vague to you. Remember, there are no "dumb questions."
4. Share your thoughts: If time and situation allows, share your personal thoughts on what you've heard. Share points that touched your own life and why you felt they were important points to remember.
5. Pray: In your personal time, pray about what you've heard on the video. Pray not only for your own clear understanding and insight, but pray for others in the group as well.

As Christians, we all desire to grow stronger in our faith and obtain a deeper understanding of God. We hope and pray this video will help you accomplish some of these goals in your own Christian journey.

The Lord's Prayer

Series Scripture Reference

In this manner, therefore, pray: Our Father in heaven, Hallowed be Your name. Your kingdom come. Your will be done on earth as it is in heaven. Give us this day our daily bread. And forgive us our debts, as we forgive our debtors. And do not lead us into temptation, ut deliver us from the evil one. For Yours is the kingdom and the power and the glory forever. Amen. Matthew 6: 9-13

Confident Faith
Session 1

"Our Father in Heaven…"

> *Now this is the confidence that we have in Him, that if we ask anything according to His will, He hears us. And if we know that He hears us, whatever we ask, we know that we have the petitions that we have asked of Him.* 1 John 5: 14-15

1. There is nothing more crippling to_____ than not having confidence in our relationship with God.

2. God as our heavenly Father is able to _____ from the broken images or painful memories of our lives.

3. In Luke 15, Jesus uses the story of the prodigal son to paint a magnificent picture of _____.

4. In this parable, Jesus has shown us how God invites us to let Him _____.

5. The Prodigal Son parable also tells us that God not only receives us as _____, but He restores us from the _____ our past has caused us.

6. We must always remember that God _____ over us!

7. What is your image of God as your heavenly Father?

DO NOT DUPLICATE THIS MATERIAL

Notes

Session 2

Transforming Faith

"Hallowed be your Name"

1. "Hallowed" literally means "_____."

2. Why is important for us to realize the throne of God is an actual place?

3. As we enter into God's presence with worship, what significant thing happens?

   But we all, with unveiled face, beholding as in a mirror the glory of the Lord, are being transformed into the same image from glory to glory, just as by the Spirit of the Lord. (2 Cor. 3:18)

4. Holiness is shown in the Bible as something relating to God's _____.

5. As we open ourselves through worship, we will find His holiness and wholeness overtaking our _____.

6. As we let our worship in His presence make us more like Him, His _____ in us will affect those around us.

7. We should move our posture in worship beyond one of _____ to one of power-filled potential for _____.

Notes

Session 3

Responsible Faith

"Your Kingdom come. Your will be done on earth as it is in Heaven."

1. "Your Kingdom come" shows us how Christ intends us to effectively discharge our _____ in prayer.

2. Jesus shows us that mankind is _____ for inviting God's rule into their heart.

3. As a race, we violated the responsibility God gave us. This betrayal began at the _____.

4. Explain God's restoration from the fall of man.

5. Explain man's responsibility.

6. With responsibility in mind, explain why Jesus instructs us to pray, "Your kingdom come?"

DO NOT DUPLICATE THIS MATERIAL

Notes

Session 4

Dependent Faith

"Give us this day our daily bread."

1. "Give us this day our daily bread," registers a specific command for us to recognize our _____ dependency on the Lord for ____ nourishment.

2. James 4:2 says, "yet you do not have because you do not ask." These words show that the Lord is ready to release many things to us—but His readiness doesn't remove our _____.

3. Dependent prayer is not _____ or _____ prayer.

4. Dependent prayer is both the _____ we gain a personal realization of God's unswerving commitment to us, and _____ we participate in God's promised provision for us.

5. "Give us today," Jesus is also showing our need to learn an _____ for each day's hours and events, as surely as our need for having adequacy of food and other needs.

6. Committing each day's details to God in prayer—requesting "today's bread"—can deliver us from _____.

7. Learning to pray, "Give us this day our daily bread," finds in the Lord a _____ proportionate to each day's needs.

DO NOT DUPLICATE THIS MATERIAL

Notes

Session 5

Releasing Faith

"And forgive us our debts, as we forgive our debtors."

1. Jesus shows us the two sides of human disobedience: sins of _____ and sins of _____, wrong things we have done and right things we neglected to do.

2. "Forgive us our debts" relates to our _____.

3. With the phrase of asking forgiveness, Christ fashions this dual dimension of release into our regular pattern of prayer: a request for release from

   _____

   _____

4. If I do not move in God's dimension of _____ toward others, I will inevitably become an obstruction to my own life, growth, and fruitfulness.

5. The prayer is not to level a focus on guilt, but on _____ .

6. Forgiveness can be counted on. The condition of _____ is presented clearly, and the availability is promised: "he can be depended on to forgive us."

7. Jesus describes forgiveness as being relayed through us _____.

8. When we go to another for reconciliation, we must be certain we are not doing so in an attempt to _____ .

9. There is no greater step upward in faith than the one we take when we learn to _____ .

   As far as the east is from the west, so far has He removed our transgressions from us. Psalm 103: 12

DO NOT DUPLICATE THIS MATERIAL

He will again have compassion on us, and will subdue our iniquities. Micah 7:19

Therefore if you bring your gift to the alter, and there remember that your brother has something against you, leave your gift there before the altar and go your way. First be reconciled to your brother, and then come and offer your gift. Matthew 5: 23-24

And whenever you stand praying, if you have anything against anyone, forgive him, that your Father in heaven may also forgive you your trespasses.
Mark 11: 25

Notes

Session 6

Obedient Faith & Trusting Faith

"And do not lead us not into temptation, but deliver us from the evil one."

1. To understand what Jesus is teaching we must first gain a clear understanding of the "temptation";
    *   First,_____
        _____
    *   Second,_____
        _____

2. Jesus isn't suggesting that we should ask or expect to avoid the kind of _____ He faced with Satan.

3. "Lead us not into temptation" is a _____ if we'll take it.

4. By the words of this prayer, we are committing ourselves in advance to _____ victory, to _____ deliverance, and to _____ the way of escape God has promised us.

    No temptation has overtaken you except such as is common to man; but God is faithful, who will not allow you to be tempted beyond what you are able, but with the temptation will also make the way of escape, that you may be able to bear it. 1 Cor 10:13

5. With "Lead us not," we come to the Lord and commit ourselves to receive _____, rather than to allow _____ to entangle us in its snares.

6. If we _____, God will deliver us out of temptation.

7. When we pray "deliver us from evil" we are committing ourselves to _____ over the things that would seek to conquer us.

DO NOT DUPLICATE THIS MATERIAL

And the Lord will deliver me from every evil work and preserve me for His heavenly kingdom.   To Him be glory forever and ever. Amen! 2 Tim 4: 18

Then the Lord knows how to deliver the godly out of temptations and to reserve the unjust under punishment for the day of judgment.   2 Peter 2: 9

Notes

Session 7

Trusting Faith

"For Yours is the kingdom and the power and the glory forever. Amen."

1. "For Yours is the kingdom and the power and the glory forever" is the active expression of a heart that has found the absolute assurance of the complete triumph of God in His _____.

    Therefore, when they had come together, they asked Him, saying, "Lord, will You at this time restore the kingdom to Israel?" And He said to them, "it is not for you to know times or seasons which the Father has put in His own authority."
    Acts 1: 6-7

    But you shall receive power when the Holy Spirit has come upon you; and you shall be witnesses to Me in Jerusalem, and in all Judea and Samaria, and to the end of the earth. Acts 1: 8

2. Jesus was showing them the Holy Spirit's coming was a mission to work the _____ of the kingdom _____ them, not the _____ of the kingdom for them.

3. Jesus was teaching the pathway to _____that He will attend to all issues.

4. Jesus is reminding us that such privileged participation in the power of His Kingdom life has terms: We are called to _____ to God's rule in our lives.

    Therefore submit to God. Resist the devil and he will flee from you. James 4: 7

    Therefore humble yourselves under the mighty hand of God, that He may exalt you in due time. 1 Peter 5: 6

5. Faith is always _____ where evil reigns.

6. In these words, "Yours is the kingdom," Jesus is leading us to realize that even though answers may not fully appear yet, two things come from trusting faith:

     • _____

     • _____

7. Explain what is meant when the Lord's Prayer concludes with, "Thine is the kingdom and the power and the glory."

8. Now that you have completed this study, list new insights you have gleaned from about the Lord's Prayer:

    a. _____

    b. _____

    c. _____

    d. _____

    e. _____

    f. _____

    g. _____

Notes

Confident Faith

In this manner, therefore, pray: Our Father in heaven, Hallowed be Your name. Your kingdom come. Your will be done on earth as it is in heaven. Give us this day our daily bread. And forgive us our debts, as we forgive our debtors. And do not lead us into temptation, but deliver us from the evil one. For Yours is the kingdom and the power and the glory forever. (Matt. 6:9-13)

Jesus opens His teaching with an emphasis on our relationship with God as "Father." In doing so, He lays the foundational truth that we are given grounds for confidence in prayer on the strength of that "Father-child" relationship, which the Bible says is established and secured through Christ.

Now this is the confidence that we have in Him, that if we ask anything according to His will, He hears us. And if we know that He hears us, whatever we ask, we know that we have the petitions that we have asked of Him. (1 John 5:14-15)

There is nothing more crippling to effective prayer than not having confidence in our relationship with God. When Jesus refers to God as the "Father," He helps us to understand the glorious relationship we are intended to have with Him.

Unfortunately, the concept of "father" has been marred for many through disappointing earthly relationships with parents or authority figures. Because of this common human fact, Jesus made a point to show us the Father in a way no one else ever could. For in Christ Himself we see that God is a Father who transcends even the finest earthly father; He is able to redeem us from the broken images or painful memories of our lives. As we follow Christ's teachings about the Father and see Him show us the Father in His life, we come to understand the power of His words to Philip: "He who has seen Me has seen the Father" (John 14:9).

In Luke 15, Jesus uses the story of the prodigal son to paint a magnificent picture of what our Father God is really like.

Here is a young man who wasted everything he'd been given – his inheritance, his opportunities, and his father's trust. He ended up working in a pigpen. But in unfolding this story, Jesus unveils God's heart toward each of us through five essential phrases. He shows that, regardless of what we have wasted, God's arms are still reaching toward us, openly and lovingly.

The first thing we learn about is God's *quest* for us. We see this in the phrase that says the father saw the prodigal son when he was still "a great way off" (v. 20). This shows us something unique and precious about the longing heart of God. For, as the father watched his wayward son, so God's heart yearns and watches for each of us, even when we are far away from Him. In other words, regardless of what we have done or where we are, *God loves us.*

Second, we see that when the father saw the son on his way home, he "had compassion, and ran and fell on his neck and kissed him" (v. 20); he *received* his son.

I have often reflected on this story, thinking about the reluctance that son must have felt as he drew closer and closer to home. He must have been uneasy about his return, feeling very unworthy. He knew he had squandered his resources, had wasted his entire inheritance, and had nearly lost his life! He had every reason to doubt his father's acceptance.

But Jesus describes God's open heart toward us by showing how the young man's father welcomed him. The verb tense used here to say, "he embraced him and kissed him" literally translates "he kissed him repeatedly." The father must have received his wandering son with much the same joy that he'd had when he first embraced him at his birth. It was as though a brand new son was being born all over again! "For this my son was dead and is alive again; he was lost and is found" (v. 24). And in this same way, it is with joy that *God receives us.*

Third, after this loving reception the Father called for "the finest robe" to be given to his son. The particular style of robe referred to was full-length in cut; in those days, a garment reserved only for those who held a position of honor and prestige. So, it is clear that this fallen son was being *restored* to his former position as an heir in the household. The privileges of relationship with his father were returned to him, even though he had lost the inheritance he'd been given. Likewise, God not only *receives* us as forgiven sons, but He *restores* us from the loss our past has caused us. Although we may have abandoned the life-gifts He first gave us, He welcomes us back with a loving embrace and brings us again to our intended place in His will and purposes.

Fourth, the father had a "jeweled ring" put on his son's finger. How the hearts of those listening to this story for the first time must have leapt when Jesus related this part! They would have recognized instantly the significance of this action, for in ancient times the giving of such a ring indicated the son's *full return to partnership* with his father in the family's business. The ring gave him the right to exercise authority in all commercial or legal matters, for it represented the full weight of whatever authority or power that family's name carried.

Thus, in calling us to pray "Our Father," Jesus has shown us how God invites us to let Him *authorize us as His partner.* Our prayer in the "family name" of Jesus is authoritative prayer. And that name is given to us freely and fully, carrying with it all the rights and privileges granted to us as members of God's eternal family.

Fifth, the Father had shoes or sandals placed on his son's feet. These shoes were more than mere clothing. Old Testament imagery teaches that people in mourning or grief commonly removed their shoes as a symbol of their sorrow. By placing shoes on his son's feet, the father was making an announcement to his son: "The time of mourning and the days of separation are over! The time of rejoicing has come!" And in this we see the final teaching of God's heart toward us: *"God rejoices over us!"* He rejoices at our return, and at the restored relationship we share with Him.

Through the story of the prodigal son, Jesus illustrates our standing before God: We are welcomed to a place of confidence through the forgiveness given to us through Christ. Our Father offers us an authoritative right to be sons (John 1:12), to function in partnership with Him and extend His dominion over all the earth. No matter what we fight, whether the powers of hell or our own weaknesses, eventual victory will be ours.

This is what Jesus wants to teach us when He instructs us to pray, "Our Father in heaven." He is founding all prayer on a growing relationship with a loving God. And as the truth of God's reception and our restoration fills us, we will discover yet another benefit: *We will learn to receive each other.* We begin, with Christ's help, to see one another as brothers and sisters who have been received by a loving Father. And in that light, we can join together in harmony, lifting up a concert of powerful, effective prayer as people who have discovered God's love and are learning to pray confidently in Him.

Transforming Faith

"HALLOWED BE YOUR NAME."

The frequently intoned word "hallowed," literally means, "Holy be Your name." In these words we are invited to experience the transforming power of prayer as Jesus introduces us to life's mightiest action: Worship. "Holy be Your name" is a call to *worship* at the throne of God.

It will better help us to understand worship when we realize that the throne of God is an actual place. We are not just offering our worship "up there somewhere." In Revelation 4:8, John describes his glorious vision of God's throne and the mighty angelic beings around it. An innumerable host is seen worshiping God, saying,

Holy, holy, holy
Lord God Almighty,
who was and is and is to come!

It is to this place that Jesus invites us, not just in an imaginary sense but in a living, dynamic sense of worship. We are called to gather before our Father and to bring Him our own offerings of praise.

Psalm 22:3 helps explain why worship is so important and so potentially transforming of our life and circumstance. The text teaches that through their worship, God's people may literally make an earthly place for Him to be enthroned in the midst of them:

Yet Thou art holy, O Thou who art enthroned upon the praises of Israel. (NASB)

Through this insight, we can see the dynamic objective of worship: it isn't simply an exercise in religious forms, but worship is God's assigned way to bring His presence and power to His people. In other words, just as *we* enter into God's presence with worship, so *He* responds by coming into our presence. Our worship invites Him to *rule* in our midst. When our hearts are opened wide in worship, God will respond. His presence and power will come to *transform*; to change us and our circumstances.

So we see a dual objective of worship: (1) To declare God's *transcendent* greatness, and (2) To receive His *transforming* power in our lives, situations, and needs.

In a dynamic sense, the words "Holy be Your name" are both an exalting of God and a humbling of ourselves. When we use those words, we are inviting the Holy Spirit to make God's presence and Person real in our midst. Such encounters on a regular basis can only bring transformation – the conforming of our wills to God's, the shaping of our lives into His likeness.

But we all, with unveiled face, beholding as in a mirror the glory of the Lord, are being transformed into the same image from glory to glory, just as by the Spirit of the Lord. (2 Cor. 3:18)

Worship is not the only means to this transformation – we need to respond to the Word, obey the Holy Spirit, and walk in obedience daily – but worship *can* bring it about faster. To better understand transformation through worshiping, let's first examine the meaning of holiness, since that is the trait of God's nature that Jesus focuses on in this section of the Lord's Prayer.

As often as "holy" is used as a worship expression, it too is seldom understood. We tend to only think of holiness as an external characteristic, a meditative expression, an organ-like tone of speech, a certain style of garments. The problem with this restrictive view is that we too easily may end in feeling intimidated or disqualified because we feel we haven't the needed external traits of holiness to earn God's pleasure.

On the other hand, some consider holiness to be a stern, forbidding trait of God's nature, a sort of attitudinal barrier on God's part – an obstacle created by His flaunting His perfection in the face of our weaknesses and sins. This too is wrong.

But in contrast, and simply stated, holiness is shown in the Bible as something relating to God's *completeness.* That is, God's holiness essentially acknowledges that *as* He is complete; there is nothing lacking in His person, and nothing needs to be added to make Him "enough." This insight into the meaning of God's holiness holds a promise: *Because* His holiness is complete, and *because* it is God's nature to give, He wants to share His holiness with us to complete *us!* His holiness, then, is not an *obstacle* to our acceptance, but a resource for our completion and fulfillment as persons. God is ready to pour Himself into us, complete those areas of our lives that are lacking or "unholy" because of our sin.

As we open ourselves through worship to this desire of God's, we will find His holiness and wholeness overtaking our *un*holiness. His personal power, responding to our worship, will begin to sweep away whatever residue remains from the destruction caused by our past sins.

In worship-filled prayer, a spiritual genetic begins to take effect. The traits and characteristics "born" into us when we became a part of God's family will begin to grow, making us more and more like Him. Just as surely as physical traits are transmitted to us by our earthly parents, so the nature and likeness of our Heavenly Father will grow in us as we learn and grow more in worshiping Him.

This truth is reflected in the command, "You must be holy, for I am holy" (Lev 11:45; 1 Peter 1:16). Those verses hold a promise of holiness and completeness. They are not so much a demand that we stretch ourselves through self-produced devices of "holiness" as they are God's guarantee that His life in us will become increasingly evident and power-fully transforming. So in teaching us this prayer, Jesus calls us into the Father's presence to give the Father the opportunity to remake us in His likeness.

That's transformation! – a transformation that allows God to extend His kingdom through us. And this personal dimension of transformation is only the beginning.

Beyond the power of worship-filled prayer to change *us,* it can also achieve a remarkable impact on *others.* In instructing us to enter the Father's presence with worship, Jesus points the way to a faith that can transform all of our lives and the lives of those we encounter. He says, "Since God is your Father, let your worship in His presence make you more like Him; and as you do, His working in you will affect those around you."

So, let us enter His presence with worship! Let's take the faith step that moves us to experience the transforming power of God's rule in our lives and character, and through our faithful prayers.

So take a new stance. Move your posture in worship beyond one of passive *reflection* to one of a power-filled potential for *transformation.* The *Holy* One we "hallow" in prayer is ready to invade each situation we address with His *completing* presence and power.

Responsible Faith

"YOUR KINGDOM COME. YOUR WILL BE DONE ON EARTH AS IT IS IN HEAVEN."

The Lord's Prayer further shows us how Christ intends us to effectively discharge our *responsibility* in prayer. "Your kingdom come. Your will be done on earth as it is in heaven." Jesus' counsel on how to pray illuminates a truth that we often ignore: People need to invite God's rule and power into the affairs of their lives through prayer, for if humans won't pray, God's rule in their circumstance is forfeited.

That thought runs counter to the common supposition, "Well, if God wants to do something, He'll just *do* it." This sorry strain of fatalism infests most minds. But the idea of man as a pawn moved by the Almighty at His whim is *totally* removed from the truth revealed in Scripture. Jesus shows us that mankind – each human being – is responsible for inviting God's rule – i.e., His benevolent purpose, presence, and power – into this world. Rather than demonstrating man as a hopeless, helpless victim of circumstance, the Bible declares that *redeemed* man is hopeful and capable of expecting victory when he prays in faith. The grounds for this understanding can be found in the beginning of the Bible. It explains why Jesus teaches us to pray for the reinstatement of God's rule "on earth as in heaven."

Man's Loss. In Genesis 1, the Bible states that dominion over this planet was given by God to man. That assignment under God's rule was not only one of great privilege, but one which essentially made mankind responsible for what would happen on earth (Gen. 1:28). Unless we understand this fact, we will never really understand that most of the confusion, agony, and distress in our world today exists as a direct result of our having betrayed God's initial entrusting of earth to us. As a race, we have violated the responsibility God gave us.

This betrayal began at the fall of man. Through that tragedy we have suffered inestimable loss. Man not only lost his *relationship* with God, but he lost his ability to *rule* responsibly as well. Man's ability and authority to successfully administrate God's rule over the earth is completely frustrated – whether the issue is environmental pollution or home and family management. And further, this lost capacity for a peaceful, healthful life has an added complication.

According to the Bible, "the whole world lies under the sway of the wicked one" (1 John 5:19). Man's fall not only lost an administration intended for us as humankind under God's rule, it also betrayed our God-given trust of ruling earth into the hands of the devil, Satan, the "Evil One." Since the Fall, mankind has not only been vulnerable to satanic deceptions, but by our own sin and rebellion we have contributed to the confused mess our world has become. Between man's sinning and Satan's hateful quest to destroy, death and destruction have invaded every part of life as we know it – breaking relationships, dashing hopes and dreams, and ruining destinies.

God's Restoration. But when man's betrayal of God's trust turned this world over to the powers of death and hell, God lovingly provided us with hope – a living option in the person of His Son. God sent Jesus, whose ministry announced the possibility of man's restoration to God's kingdom: "Repent, for the kingdom of heaven is at hand" (Matt. 4:17). In that statement, Jesus made it clear that the rule of God was once again being made available to mankind. No longer did any member of the race need to remain a hopeless victim of sin and hell!

In His ministry, both then and now, Jesus manifests every aspect of the kingdom He offers. When Jesus heals, He is showing what can happen when the rule of God enters a situation. When He answers need at any dimension, He is putting into action the power of God's rule available for our lives. As Jesus teaches, His objective has always been to help straighten out our thinking ("repent"), to help us see what Father God is really like, so that we might respond correctly to Him and His kingdom.

But at the same time that Jesus ministers, hell seeks to level its hostile devices against the Messiah King and the kingdom He offers. Consequently, Jesus demonstrates a warlike *opposition* to the invisible powers of darkness. He is well known for demonstrating God's love, but He is equally well known for the way He confronts the demonic powers of hell. Colossians 2:15 says that in the climactic act of His crucifixion, Christ smashed these powers, (1) making possible the offer of reentry into divine life with God, and (2) paving the way for us, His followers, to also strike down satanic powers we encounter (Mark 16:17-20).

Man's Responsibility. In light of these truths, each person must decide whether or not he or she will draw on the resources of Christ's triumph through the cross and learn to live to advance God's kingdom in this world. Acceptance of Christ *begins* our participation in His Kingdom (John 3:3-5), and we are then called to *advance* it, as we share the gospel of Christ with the world around us (Matt. 28:19; Acts 1:8). There is no more effective way to accelerate this advance than for believers to pray together!

Our *first steps* in faith are made on the feet of prayer, whether we are moving into victory or into witness. Our ongoing growth in prayer is in our recognizing that faith and victory are *not* achieved merely through the zeal of human programs, but by power-prayer that acknowledges Calvary's triumph as a release for God's presence and power.

This is why Jesus instructs us to pray "Your kingdom come." By this prayer we are taking on our role as members of a race who once betrayed the King and forfeited His intended purposes into the claws of the adversary. But now, as His redeemed sons and daughters, He has endowed us with restored "kingdom authority," through prayer to welcome His entry into every need and pain of this planet.

The power is God's, but the privilege *and* responsibility to pray are ours. So, let us hear and understand Jesus' words and come together at His throne, expecting and receiving the flow of the Holy Spirit's power. By His anointing we will find prayer enablement to see God's purposes being accomplished through us.

This is what it means to pray, "Thy kingdom come;" to see the rule and power of the kingdom of God as present and practical, to see the personal possibilities for power-prayer in every dimension of our daily lives. Never let the promise of Christ's future kingdom keep us from possessing the dimensions of victory that God has for us *now*. Jesus is coming again to establish His kingdom over all the earth! But that should not cause us to neglect our present prayer or ministry responsibilities for advancing the Gospel.

Until He comes again, Jesus directed us to "occupy" (Luke 19:13, KJV). That "occupation" entails drawing on the resources of God's kingdom and power, reaching into the realm of the invisible through prayer, and changing one circumstance after another.

"Your kingdom come. Your will be done on earth as it is in heaven." It is our privilege to pray this, and our responsibility thereby to exercise the beginning of our reinstatement to partnership with God, in seeing the tangled affairs of this planet reversed from the fallen order to God's intended order.

Dependent Faith

"GIVE US THIS DAY OUR DAILY BREAD."

In these words, Jesus is talking about more than our having enough food or having our physical needs met. He is issuing an invitation for us to come to the Father daily for refreshing, for renewal and nourishment for both our souls and our bodies. This phrase, "Give us this day our daily bread," registers a specific command for us to recognize our *dependency* on the Lord for *all* nourishment, and to realize that this provision for our needs flows out of the discipline of daily prayer.

James 4:2 makes a strong statement regarding the necessity of prayer: "Yet you do not have because you do not ask." These words show that the Lord is ready to release many things to us – but His readiness doesn't remove our place or need of asking. In other words, the promises or prophecies of God's care for us do not bypass our need for prayerful, acknowledged dependence. The Lord Jesus teaches us to willingly turn to the Father and call out in prayer for Him to work in our lives. Rather than relying on our own strength (chin up, teeth clenched: "I'm going to get this done."), we need to come to the Father in prayer. Daily. Dependently. And gratefully.

Dependent prayer is not desperate or demeaning prayer. It is neither frantic (as though we only resorted to turning to God in a crisis) nor depersonalizing (as though God required us to grovel in order to escape His wrath). In contrast to these distorted views, dependent prayer is both the *way* we gain a personal realization of God's unswerving commitment *to* us, and *how* we participate in God's promised provision *for* us.

Psalm 80:12 says, "So teach us to number our days, that we may gain a heart of wisdom." It's a sound minded request for wisdom to recognize how *few* days we have, and how much we need to employ them wisely. In the words, "Give us today," Jesus is showing our need to learn an accountability for each day's hours and events, as surely as our need for having adequacy of food and other needs. Dependent prayer can help us do this. Jesus is not merely teaching us to request "bread" at morning, noon, and night. He is teaching us to ask for the Father's direction and provision in every event and during each hour of our day.

Committing each day's details to God in prayer – requesting "today's bread" – can deliver us from pointless pursuits and wasted time. Such prayer paves the way to victorious days. "My times are in Your hand; deliver me from the hand of my enemies (Ps. 31:15).

What wisdom! When we put our day in God's hands, any enemy we face can be conquered. Whether our enemy is ourselves – procrastination, sloth, or other weaknesses – or the enemy is a demonic conspiracy Satan has plotted against us, *our Lord is able to deliver us!* "Daily bread" praying is "daily victory" and "daily overcoming" praying, because it enters into drawing on God's full provision for our sufficiency. He will help us overcome anything that might wrench our lives from his purpose, or cause valuable time to slip through our fingers.

Submit your day to the Lord and ask Him to provide for your needs. Whether your need is food or counsel for the day's activities, you will find that it *will* be provided. He will faithfully and abundantly respond as we set our "times" in His hands.

And when we learn to pray this way we will find another wonderful promise being fulfilled: "As your days, so shall your strength be" (Deut. 33:25). Learning to pray, "Give us this day our daily bread," finds in the Lord a strength proportionate to each day's needs. Whatever challenges a day holds – confrontations, difficulties, even tragedies – we will receive the strength to face it. Just as we derive physical strength and nourishment from eating daily bread, so we will gain spiritual strength and nourishment when we learn the wisdom of acknowledging our dependency upon the Father – and pray His way.

Releasing Faith

"AND FORGIVE US OUR DEBTS, AS WE FORGIVE OUR DEBTORS."

The next point in the Lord's Prayer addresses our need for forgiveness. Some people use the phrase "trespass against us," while others use the word "debts" for this section of the prayer. Both expressions are accurate and uniquely significant. In fact, we need to pray *both* ways, for in these two expressions Jesus shows us the two sides of human disobedience: sins of *commission* and sins of *omission,* wrong things we have done and right things we neglected to do.

"Forgive us our trespasses" speaks to our need of asking the Lord to forgive us for having "stepped over the line." God is concerned about trespassing because He wants to keep us from the things which will damage or destroy us. In his Word He sets clear, protective guidelines – territorial boundaries, if you will – that say, "Do not trespass here." When we violate these commands intended to help us avoid what becomes self-destructive, we are guilty of "sins of commission."

On the other hand, "Forgive us our debts" relates to our failures; to cases where it might be said that we "owed it" to the situation to do differently than we did. But in failing to act rightly, we have become debtors. And such indebtedness can hang like a cloud over the soul, hindering our sense of freedom and faith for the future.

With this phrase of asking forgiveness, Christ fashions this dual dimension of release into our regular pattern of prayer: a request for release from (1) the shame of guilt, or (2) the pain of neglect.

To grasp the power potential in this prayer for forgiveness, we need to see that both of the phrases are conditionally linked. In saying, "as we forgive," Jesus specifically teaches that the degree of our forgiveness – our willingness to release others – establishes a standard of measurement. He gives back to us that measure of release and forgiveness that we show others. And this fact brings us to the heart of life's most practical truth: *If I do not move in God's dimension of release and forgiveness toward others, I will inevitably become an obstruction to my own life, growth, and fruitfulness.*

See it, dear one. There are dual dimensions. We need to see that "forgiving faith" goes both ways: (1) We must confess our own sinning; and (2) We must forgive others whom we feel violate us.

Notice also, that by emphasizing our need for forgiveness of sin, Jesus isn't shaking a stick of condemnation in our faces. This isn't the issue. The real problem is that we are all somewhat warped and need to be *taught* to pray for forgiveness. We are all people *bent* from God's original design and purpose. Not one of us is flawless, no one without selfishness and pride. Sin is an inherited inclination in us all, and it needs to be forgiven. The call to pray this prayer is the promise it will be answered. We *need* to pray, "Forgive me, Father," and we need to pray it often. But the prayer is *not* to level a focus on guilt, but on grace.

Jesus taught us to pray for forgiveness on a regular basis, not to remind us of our sinfulness but to keep us from becoming sloppy in our ideas about the grace of God. Too often, we distort God's grace and give in to the deception that "I can do anything I want as long as God's grace encompasses me." But in Roman's 6:1-2, the Word demands pointedly: "What shall we say then? Shall we continue in sin that grace may abound?

Certainly not! How shall we who died to sin live any longer in it?" In calling us to pray, "Forgive us our trespasses," Jesus isn't seeking to remind us of our failures, but He *does* want to sensitize us to sin, and to the fact that this sin hinders our growth in Him.

God's forgiveness is graciously offered and abundantly available. He warmly invites us to pardon, cleansing, and release in the Scriptures:

- As far as the east is from the west, so far has He removed our transgressions from us. (PS. 103:12)
- He will again have compassion on us, and will subdue our iniquities. (MICAH 7:19)
- Their sins and their lawless deeds I will remember no more. (HEB. 10:17)
- If we confess our sins, He is faithful and just to forgive us our sins and to cleanse us from all unrighteousness. (1 JOHN 1:9)

Forgiveness can be counted on. The condition – *confession* – is presented clearly, and the availability is promised: "He can be depended on to forgive us."

Second, Jesus describes forgiveness as being relayed *through* us to others. God's Word expands and applies the truth that we who have received forgiveness need to be forgiving. Jesus directs us to go to anyone who has something against us and, in an attitude of humility and forgiveness, rectify our relationship with them. And He says this must be done before we can make any serious, honest approach to Him in worship.

Therefore if you bring your gift to the altar, and there remember that your brother has something against you, leave your gift there before the altar and go your way. First be reconciled to your brother, and then come and offer your gift. (Matt. 5:23-24)

And whenever you stand praying, if you have anything against anyone, forgive him, that your Father in heaven may also forgive you your trespasses. (Mark 11:25)

When we go to another for reconciliation, we must be certain we are not doing so in an attempt to justify ourselves. If someone has a difference of opinion or some problem with me, regardless of whose fault it is, God will not allow me to make any charge against that person. Christ desires that we be willing to go the extra mile and assume the role of reconciler – just as He did for us in reconciling us to the Father.

Understanding that people often perceive a situation opposite of how it really is will help us act as Christ commands. For example, if you have been offended, you may be completely unaware of the viewpoint of the one you feel has hurt you. To the other person, it will often seem as though *he* or *she* were the one violated, and that *you* are at fault. The effects of sin and Satan's discord in our lives makes us all *so* terribly vulnerable to natural misunderstandings, we need to learn this point of human understanding. We must acknowledge it in order to open up the reconciling process. Then when we become willing to go to others, recognizing that their attitudes toward us are likely based on something they perceive as being *our* fault – when *we* accept the burden of the misunderstanding (as Jesus did to bring peace between God and us), a real release *will be realized*. Let's learn to accept the responsibility for whatever has breached our relationships with others. Restored relationships can become possible when this Christlike lifestyle lives out the meaning in His prayer lesson: "Forgive *me*…as I forgive others."

Naturally, there may be times when the most loving, scriptural stand we can take is to confront others with their wrong. Jesus did so, and the Holy Spirit will show us when we are to do so. But the Spirit of forgiveness never does this in a self-defensive way; rather it operates in a spirit of reconciliation.

This kingdom order of forgiveness will not always be easy.

By nature we all prefer to be "in the driver's seat," so to speak, and the ministry of "reconciliation" always puts us at the mercy of the *other's* responses instead. But this is exactly where Jesus put Himself when He laid down His life to offer forgiveness to us. Though God hasn't called us to be someone's doormat, we *are* called to learn Christ's pathway to dominion. To do so is to see that this kingdom path to power is in the Spirit of the Lamb, and never in one of self defense.

There is no greater step upward in faith than the one we take when we learn to forgive – and *do it*. It blesses people who need our love and acceptance, and it releases us to bright horizons of joy, health, and dynamic faith in prayer.

Obedient Faith

"AND DO NOT LEAD US NOT INTO TEMPTATION, BUT DELIVER US FROM THE EVIL ONE."

Our sixth step brings us to the most paradoxical part of the Lord's Prayer: "And do not lead us into temptation, but deliver us from the evil one." At first these words seem confusing in light of other Scriptures which assure us that God does not tempt anyone. James 1:13-14 makes this clear: "God tempts no man, but when we are tempted we are drawn away of our own lusts and enticed." Seeing this, then, we know that in teaching us to pray, "Lead us not into temptation," Jesus is not teaching us that we have to beg God not to trick us into sinning. Nor is Jesus teaching us a prayer for escaping the demands of growth that come through God's leading us – and He *does* lead us – into *trial.*

To understand what Jesus is teaching we must first gain a clear understanding of the word "temptation;" a word that carries a two-sided meaning. First, temptation essentially has to do with the desire of an adversary to test and break through our defenses. Second, temptation deals with the strength gained through encountering an adversary; that is, when the one who is tested overcomes the test, the resulting victory builds strength. Temptation, therefore, is both positive and negative, depending on our viewpoint and response.

In that light, Jesus isn't suggesting that we should ask or expect to avoid the kind of confrontation He faced with Satan. In fact, the Bible tells us that the Holy Spirit *led* Christ into that experience of conflict with the devil (Matt. 4:1). As a direct result of overcoming this time of temptation, Jesus was brought to a place of victory and dominion over the enemy (John 14:30). So this section of the Lord's Prayer holds a promise of victory, rather than a plea for relief from struggle.

We are not asking God, "Please don't play with us as pawns on a chessboard, risking our loss by 'leading us' into questionable situations." Rather, to examine various translations of this challenging verse and noting the tense and mood of the Greek verb *lead* or *bring unto,* is to discover the phrase "Lead us not into temptation" is a *guarantee of victory* – if we'll take it!

A clear translation of these words shows Jesus is actually directing us to pray: "Father, should we at any point be led into temptation, test, or trial, we want to come out delivered and victorious."

So the issue in this portion of the Lord's Prayer is not a questioning of God's character, but *ours.* Such praying is saying, "Lord, *You* won't lead or introduce me into any situations but those for my refinement, growth, and victory. Therefore, when I encounter circumstances designed to lead me astray, I *will* recognize that it *isn't* Your will for me to walk that way. By the words of this prayer, God, I am committing myself in advance to *wanting* victory, to *seeking* deliverance, and to *taking* the way of escape You have promised me."

No temptation has overtaken you except such as is common to man; but God is faithful, who will not allow you to be tempted beyond what you are able, but with the temptation will also make the way of escape, that you may be able to bear it. (1 COR. 10:13)

Here, then, is obedient faith confronting the reality of our vulnerability to temptation. It's sometimes so quick in its rise and so subtle in its approach that Jesus' prayer lesson teaches us our need to have established our steps in advance through regular prayer. With these words, "Lead us not," we come to the Lord, in advance, and commit ourselves to receive His deliverances, rather than to allow temptation to entangle us in its snares. This prayer doesn't question God's nature or leading, but declares we are casting ourselves on Him.

Once again, it's important to understand the intent of this prayer because man is so easily deluded by temptation. Jesus isn't suggesting it is God's nature to trick or corrupt us by tempting us. Instead He's emphasizing it is God's nature to "deliver us from evil." The prayer simply establishes a commitment on our part to receive the triumphant life Christ offers us in dominion over evil. Living becomes more effective when we avoid being neutralized by hell's manipulations or by our flesh's cry for self-indulgence.

This prayer doesn't remove temptation's challenge, but it does help us understand that we aren't evil simply because we're tempted. Furthermore, we have a certain promise: God has a doorway of exit for us! When temptation comes, the prayer "deliver us from evil" insures us a way out.

What a great certainty this is. What a beautiful climax to this lesson in the Lord's Prayer.

And the Lord will deliver me from every evil work and preserve me for His heavenly kingdom. To Him be glory forever and ever. Amen! (2 TIM. 4:18)

Then the Lord knows how to deliver the godly out of temptations and to reserve the unjust under punishment for the day of judgment. (2 PETER 2:9)

If we seek Him, God *will* deliver us out of temptation! Thus, when we pray "deliver us from evil" we are committing ourselves to walk in triumph and dominion over the things that would seek to conquer us: to live in obedient faith. And to live this way is to count on God's deliverance, for "He is able!"

Trusting Faith

"FOR YOURS IS THE KINGDOM AND THE POWER AND THE GLORY FOREVER. AMEN."

Our study of the Lord's Prayer is climaxed in examining these words of trusting faith: "For Yours is the *kingdom* and the *power* and the *glory* forever." Here is the active expression of a heart that has found the absolute assurance of the complete triumph of God…in *His* time.

Turn with me to Acts 1:6-7. I think the words of Jesus to His disciples will give us additional insight into this section of the Lord's Prayer:

> Therefore, when they had come together, they asked Him, saying, "Lord, will You at this time restore the kingdom to Israel?"
> And He said to them, "It is not for you to know times or seasons which the Father has put in His own authority."

Jesus spoke these words following His resurrection, as He was giving His final instructions to His men before His ascension. He had been explaining principles of the kingdom of God, and the disciples had gotten confused (Acts 1:3-5). In light of what He was teaching, and with the facts of the Crucifixion and the Resurrection behind them, Jesus' disciples inquired: "Just when will this kingdom finally come?" They must have felt sure ("Surely, now!") since Jesus was continuing to speak of the kingdom now (Acts 1:3) *after* His death as He had *before* His death, that the time *must* be ripe for the messianic kingdom to be established. Surely now was the time for Israel to be liberated from Roman oppression!

But Jesus patiently replied that it wasn't for them to know when it would take place (v. 7). He wasn't stalling them. Nor was He denying the ultimate kingdom someday. But He was redirecting their understanding. The issue of the kingdom's "coming with power" is asserted in the very next verse:

But you shall receive power when the Holy Spirit has come upon you; and you shall be witnesses to Me in Jerusalem, and in all Judea and Samaria, and to the end of the earth. (ACTS 1:8)

He was showing them the Holy Spirit's coming was a mission to work the *spread* of the kingdom *through* them, not the *finish* of the kingdom *for* them. This conversation between Jesus and His disciples, with Jesus' promise of the Holy Spirit's power in relation to the timing of His kingdom, can help us understand the meaning of the concluding phrase of the Lord's Prayer. We can see that Jesus was teaching the pathway to *trust* – to the knowledge that when we have prayed in faith, we can rest firm in our confidence God has heard – He *will* attend to all issues, and even when we don't see *our* timing in the answer, *His* purposes aren't being lost.

Consider the words, "Thine is the kingdom."

For many, these words seem to point to the future. But Jesus taught very clearly that in certain respects the presence and power of His kingdom are given to us *now:* "Do not fear, little flock, for it is your Father's good pleasure to give you the kingdom" (Luke 12:32). Although we will only experience the *fullest* expression of His kingdom when He comes again, we mustn't diminish the fact that this prayer is dealing with God's rule and power impacting situations *now*. Wherever the Spirit is given room and allowed to work, the kingdom "comes."

So here, at prayer, Jesus is reminding us that such privileged participation in the power of His kingdom life has terms: We are called to submit to God's rule in our lives.

Therefore submit to God. Resist the devil and he will flee from you. (JAMES 4:7)

Therefore humble yourselves under the mighty hand of God, that He may exalt you in due time. (1 PETER 5:6)

The Power and the Glory

The first factor in developing a trusting faith is learning that the rule, the power, and the glory *are* God's. He allows us to share with Him, but He is Lord. He gives us power, but only He is omnipotent. He teaches us, but He alone is all-knowing. And the submitting and humbling spoken of in James and 1 Peter are prerequisites to sharing God's authority. Satan flees the believer who has learned the truth of *"Yours* is the power."

Faith is ever and always challenging the status quo where evil reigns, where pain and sickness prevail, where hatred and hellishness rule, or where human failure breeds confusion. As we learn to live under the Holy Spirit's rule, we will be able to take a bold, confrontive stance against all in opposition to that rule – whether demon, flesh, or earthly circumstance. Such a stance says, "I rely upon the One who claims ultimate and final rule everywhere. I won't give way to any lie which attempts to cast doubt on God's ultimate, complete victory." And when we do this, we will often see results which would not have been realized without "kingdom praying."

But what about when we don't see any results?

What then?

The disciples' inquiry echoes from our lips too: "Will the kingdom be now?"

To this question, Jesus teaches us to pray, *"Yours is the kingdom."* In these words He's leading us to realize that even though answers may not fully appear yet, two things come from trusting faith: (1) The knowledge that the ultimate triumph of God's manifest power shall come *in His time;* and (2) The assurance that, *until that time,* He has given us His Spirit to enable us to do His will.

Here is our fortress of confidence. Although time may pass without our always seeing "victory" as we would interpret it, we know – and pray with praise – we have not been deserted! God's Holy Spirit brings us His presence and power right now, for whatever circumstances we encounter.

There will be times we will see God's kingdom power in action – in healings and miracles in our lives. And there will also be times the Lord simply says, "Trust Me – the time is not yet, but in the meantime the power of My Spirit will sustain you,"

Great power and privilege *are* given to the church. "Nothing will be impossible for you," Jesus says (Matt. 17:20). Yet, as certain as the promise and possibilities are, we must humbly and honestly acknowledge there are some times when we seem unable to "possess" the promise. Such acknowledgments should not seem to be statements of doubt. Nor are they cases of God's refusing to grant us an answer or fulfill His Word.

God's promises *are* true and His Word *is* faithful! But the "kingdom timing" is His too! And so are the ultimate power and glory.

When we conclude the Lord's Prayer with, "Thine is the kingdom and the power and the glory," we aren't being either passive or poetic. We are reflecting the power of trusting faith: faith which stands in firm confidence, regardless of circumstances. This faith declares, "Lord to You belongs all kingdom authority, You are the possessor of all! And as I gain that kingdom, a portion at a time, I trust You – for the kingdom is Yours."

There are no greater grounds for rest and contentment in life than the certainty wrapped in these words:

"Yours is the kingdom" – all rule *belongs* to God.

"Yours is the power" – all mightiness *flows* from Him.

"Yours is the glory" – His victory *shall be* complete.

With this kind of prayer comes boldness, confidence, and rest. For when all is said and done, our greatest resource is to rest in God's greatness. In Him we find confidence that our every need will be met, our ultimate victory realized; and in His time, by His purpose, and for His glory, all things will resolve unto His wisest, richest, and best.

So let us, now and ever, join the angelic throng around His throne, uniting our concert of prayer and praise with theirs, saying, "Holy, holy, holy...

Who was.

Who is.

And Who is to come –

THE ALMIGHTY!

The EZ Lesson Plan

To purchase these other new products visit your local Christian bookstore, call our toll free number 800-933-9673, extension #92039 or visit our website at **www.nelsonword.com**

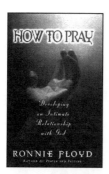

HOW TO PRAY   BY: DR. RONNIE FLOYD

Dr. Floyd teaches us not only How To Pray, but the meaning of Prayer, intercessory prayer, world prayer, prayer for illness and Most importantly heart felt prayer. Four sessions complete with All the tools you will need to teach the class.

GOD IS FAITHFUL   BY: SHEILA WALSH

Sheila Walsh teaches a small group how to cope with the grief complications of our everyday life. Why we should turn to God in not only our personal times of need but for our friends, church and all around us. A new design in women's study.

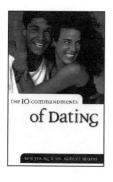

TEN COMMANDMENTS OF DATING
BY: BEN YOUNG AND SAM ADAMS

What are you doing for those in your church that are....

Singled by choice or change?

Every church has the same problem of finding the material to fit the over all needs of being single. This program teaches how to cope with all aspects of single life from sex to sin and sixteen to sixty. A must for your singles ministry.

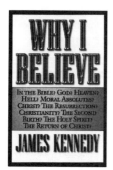

WHY I BELIEVE   BY: D. JAMES KENNEDY

A study taken from the greatest works of all....THE BIBLE.
Dr. Kennedy explains how truth conquers all and needs no explanation.
Why we should believe in God, Jesus Christ, the birth, death and resurrection.

Video Curriculum Series

Please visit your local Christian bookstore, call our toll free number 800-933-9673, extension 92039 or visit our website at www.nelsonword.com to inquire about our new video assisted programs. These are all very affordable and done by names you have learned to trust over the years.

Seven Promises Practiced – A video assisted series from Promise Keepers for the men in your church. *Chuck Swindoll, Max Lucado, Gary Smalley* and a host of others teach on the *Seven Great Promises* of a Promise Keeper and how they should be practiced. These great communicators explain A Man and His Church, A Man and His God, A Man and His Brother and four more outstanding messages.

E Quake – Pastor Jack Hayford

Unlocking the Book of Revelation is a study that not only makes the study of Revelation informative, but it also brings hope and pleasure to this great scripture. Now in nine full sessions, Pastor Hayford clearly describes the end of times and how to interpret it.

21 Laws of Leadership – John C. Maxwell

"Your church will never rise above the level of your leadership," says John Maxwell to a group of one thousand pastors. Princess Diana applied just the *Law of Influence* and was loved by millions while her husband could not persuade people to give him the time of day. This program will bring new meaning to the word "leadership".

The Road to Armageddon...and Beyond
By Chuck Swindoll, John Walvoord, Dwight Pentecost, etc.

This six part series comes from a great study done by *Chuck Swindoll* and a group of astute professors teaching on End Of Times. No...they do not say it is coming in this year, but they will assure you it is coming...and how you and your church should prepare. Do all of your members understand the end of times will be a glorious occasion and not a day of gloom and doom? Bring these great professors to your church for only a fraction of what the real cost would be and...the best is experiencing them.